PENGUIN BOOKS

Country Women's A

Family Meals

Country Women's Association

Family Meals

TRADITIONAL, TEMPTING, TRIED-AND-TRUE

PENGUIN BOOKS

Contents

Foreword

The Country Women's Association of Australia has been in existence for more than 80 years and its members have long had a reputation for being wonderful cooks. Indeed, too often it seems that the public and the media think that our main activity is 'making tea and scones', though this is far from the case. But it is true that cooking and catering by our members, especially at local agricultural shows, have always been a major source of fundraising, enabling the CWA to raise many hundreds of thousands of dollars over the years, which has been used to support families and communities particularly in rural areas.

The recipes in this series of cookbooks reflect the way in which our pioneer women used the simple ingredients they had to hand to make nutritious snacks, soups, stews, sweets and cakes, and would ensure their household a year-round supply of jams, jellies and relishes by preserving fruit when it was in season. Some of these recipes are family favourites and have been handed down through the generations, being adapted along the way to suit the available ingredients and local conditions. Many members have also adopted and adapted 'new' foods introduced to Australia from other countries.

We are proud to be working with Penguin Books in putting together these cookbooks and to be sharing with you our members' prized recipes. In so doing, once again CWA members are providing a valuable service to rural communities, as the royalties from the series (and from the recipe book *Country Classics*, which was republished by Penguin in 2007) will help us fund a postgraduate nursing scholarship. This is awarded to a nurse working in a rural area, allowing them to learn new skills and thus continue to provide an essential service to their community.

The scholarship is of especial importance as we see the nation's health services struggling – in all parts of Australia, but particularly in rural communities where sometimes the nurse is the only health professional available.

May you get as much pleasure from trying these recipes as the members of the Country Women's Association have in sharing them with you.

Lesley Young
National President (2006–2009)
Country Women's Association of Australia

MASONS

About the CWA

The Country Women's Association was established in Australia during the early 1920s, in New South Wales. A conference was organised in Sydney in 1922 to coincide with the Easter Show, a time when many rural women 'came to town' with their families. There were increasing shared concerns about the issues facing women and their families in rural communities, and as well as agreeing on various social and political objectives the conference saw a committee formed to establish an organisation to promote the interests of women on the land. The idea was not new, as rural women's organisations had been around for many years in other parts of the world, the first recorded group having been formed in Finland in the 1700s.

Following the formation of this first CWA branch, many more spread throughout New South Wales and in other states. By the late 1930s there were CWA offices in all states and territories of Australia. During World War II the associations contributed in a number of ways to the war effort: local branches made their rooms and other facilities available and produced food, entertainment, equipment and clothing for Australian servicemen. They also helped the many women who were left behind to run the family farm while their husbands were away at the war.

In 1945 the state associations agreed to form a national body, the Country Women's Association of Australia. The first national meeting was held in Adelaide in 1946. Since those early days, our members have continued to support rural families and have lobbied governments on all sorts of matters including education, health, transport, aged care, child care and libraries. They have also addressed broader issues such as commodity prices, farm safety, GM crops, and water.

We are part of a world organisation of more than 9 million members in about 70 countries, the Associated Country Women of the World. The funds raised from our 'tea and scones' and other enterprises have allowed us to support many people in many different ways, not just in the country but throughout Australia and also overseas, including our sister members in the South Pacific.

At home, the range and scope of our activities have been of particular importance during the recent drought years, with money being donated from all levels of government and from corporations such as Woolworths (through their 'Drought Days' program), Bega Cheese and many others, for us to distribute to affected families. We have been able to pay families' emergency household expenses, have held community get-togethers, and have also supported other rural organisations. In addition to drought, some areas have experienced extreme and devastating rains and bushfires, and our branches have been able to assist, from their own emergency funds, those suffering hardship as a result.

Today we have some 44000 members in 1855 branches country-wide. Even though our membership numbers are dwindling, I am confident that the Country Women's Association of Australia will continue to support rural communities for at least another 80 years. If you are interested in helping us with this work, we encourage you to join up – there will be a branch near you. Give your state office a call and see how you can become part of an organisation that cares for families not only in rural and remote areas but throughout Australia.

Small meals, snacks and starters

Gingered chicken wings

I usually serve these chicken wings alongside other savoury items.

JOYCE GOOS, VALENTINE PLAINS BRANCH, QLD

1 kg chicken wings (about 12 wings)

⅓ cup soy sauce

1 tablespoon lime juice

1 tablespoon lemon juice

1 teaspoon ground ginger

2 teaspoons honey

2 tablespoons tomato sauce

SERVES 3–4

Cut the tips off the chicken wings and cut each wing into two pieces. Place in a bowl.

Combine the soy sauce, lime and lemon juices, ginger, honey and tomato sauce to make a marinade, and pour it over the wings. Cover and marinate for several hours in the fridge (or overnight).

Remove wings from the marinade (reserving marinade) and grill or barbecue on medium–high heat for about 10 minutes. Brush wings with reserved marinade, turn over and grill the other side for 10 minutes.

Spaghetti scones

ANITA MORRISH, VICTORIA HILL BRANCH, QLD

- 170 g self-raising flour
- 110 g wholemeal self-raising flour
- salt
- about 80 g shortening
- 1 × 420-g can spaghetti in tomato sauce
- 1 dessertspoon Worcestershire sauce
- 1 egg, beaten
- milk, for glazing

MAKES 10–14

Preheat the oven to 200°C. Grease a baking tray.

Sift together flours and salt, then rub in shortening to make crumbs. Add spaghetti, Worcestershire sauce and egg and mix to a soft dough. Turn dough onto a floured board and knead until smooth. Roll out and cut into scone rounds with a biscuit cutter. Place on prepared tray and brush tops with milk. Bake for 10–12 minutes.

Sally's potato bake

ELAINE YOUD, DEVONPORT BRANCH, TAS.

- 4 medium-sized potatoes, sliced (unpeeled)
- 1 clove garlic, crushed
- 3 rashers bacon (or use bacon pieces)
- 1 large onion, sliced
- 1 cup crumbled gruyere cheese

SERVES 4–6

Preheat the oven to 200°C. Grease a gratin dish.

Rub potatoes with garlic and layer in a dish with the bacon and onion. Scatter cheese on top. Bake for 30 minutes, until potatoes are tender.

Indian salad

This salad is very refreshing.

AILSA BOND A.M., RIVERSIDE BRANCH, TAS.

1 small carrot, diced
1 red capsicum, diced
1 green capsicum, diced
½ cucumber, diced
1 tomato, diced
1 red onion, diced
1 chilli, finely chopped
7 coriander stems, finely chopped
handful fresh mint, finely chopped
lemon juice, to taste

SERVES 6

Combine all ingredients in a large bowl, squeeze lemon juice over and mix well.

Savoury filled cob loaf

I make this lovely recipe when I have people coming for dinner – instead of an entrée I serve this with drinks and other nibbles.

WENDY WHITE, DARWIN BRANCH, NT

- 1 round loaf of bread
- 1 × 250-g packet cream cheese
- 300 ml light cream
- 3 rashers bacon, cooked and chopped
- chopped spring onions, to taste
- 2 cups grated cheese

SERVES 6–8

Preheat the oven to 180°C.

Neatly cut off the top of the loaf and set aside. Pull out the soft bread inside the loaf, breaking it into pieces about the size of a twenty-cent piece. Either leave the bread pieces fresh or bake them in the oven until golden-brown.

To make the dip, mix the cream cheese with the light cream until smooth. Mix in the bacon, spring onions and grated cheese. Spoon mixture into the hollow loaf and place the top back on. Wrap the loaf in aluminium foil and bake for 1–1½ hrs. Serve with the pieces of bread on the side for dipping.

Fried rice

HELEN WALL, CANIAMBO BRANCH, VIC.

1 tablespoon oil

1 large onion, chopped

3–4 rashers bacon, chopped

1 cup rice

1 egg

1 cup mixed vegetables (peas, beans, corn kernels)

2 chicken stock cubes

3 cups hot water

soy sauce, to taste

SERVES 2–4

Heat oil in a pan and fry the onion, bacon and rice until browned. Clear a space in the centre, crack in the egg and fry until cooked. Remove egg, chop, and combine with the vegetables.

Add the crumbled stock cubes, hot water and vegetable mix to the pan with the rice and simmer until rice and vegetables are cooked and all the water has been absorbed. Season to taste with soy sauce.

Curried scallops

M. M. STACKHOUSE, YARRAM BRANCH, VIC.

8–12 fresh scallops, washed
1 cup milk, plus a little extra
1 tablespoon butter
2 tablespoons cornflour
1 teaspoon curry powder

SERVES 2 AS A MAIN OR 4 AS AN ENTRÉE

Place scallops in a heatproof bowl, cover with boiling water and let stand for 20 minutes.

In a saucepan, heat the milk with the butter. Make a paste of the cornflour, curry powder and a little milk, then mix into the heated milk and stir over low heat until thickened. Pour sauce over the drained scallops, and serve immediately. (For a main course, serve alongside some cooked vegetables.)

Warm roasted vegetables

I would say I make this recipe at least once a week. It was given to me by a friend when I was trying – I say 'trying'! – to diet. You can use any vegetables you like.

WENDY WHITE, DARWIN BRANCH, NT

300 g butternut pumpkin or sweet potato, peeled and chopped into 2-cm cubes

2 potatoes, peeled and chopped into 2-cm cubes

1 capsicum, chopped into large pieces

1 zucchini, chopped into large pieces

1 carrot, chopped into large pieces

1 onion, quartered

100 g mushrooms, quartered

olive or canola oil spray

dressing

1 tablespoon balsamic vinegar

1 teaspoon olive oil

1 tablespoon honey

1 tablespoon chopped fresh basil

SERVES 4

Preheat the oven to 220°C. Line a large baking tray with baking paper.

Place pumpkin and potato in a microwave-safe dish with a little water, cover with a lid and cook on HIGH for about 4 minutes. Drain.

Toss pumpkin and potato with the capsicum, zucchini, carrot, onion and mushrooms, then spread over the prepared tray. Spray lightly with oil and bake in the oven for 30–40 minutes, turning every 15 minutes.

Mix all dressing ingredients in a small bowl.

When vegetables are cooked, place in a serving dish and pour the dressing over.

Vietnamese salad

AILSA BOND A.M., RIVERSIDE BRANCH, TAS.

- 2 tablespoons sugar
- 1 small cup boiling water
- ½ cup oil
- ⅓ cup brown vinegar
- 2 × 80-g packets chicken-flavour instant noodles
- 2 sticks celery
- 6 spring onions
- ½ head cabbage
- 8 tablespoons toasted sesame seeds, to serve
- fresh Vietnamese mint, parsley or coriander (optional)

SERVES 6

Dissolve sugar in the boiling water, then add oil, vinegar and chicken flavour sachets. Break up noodles, pour liquid over and leave to soak while you chop the celery and spring onions, and shred the cabbage. Add vegetables to the noodles, stir, then set aside for 1–2 hours before serving.

Scatter salad with sesame seeds to serve. Fresh herbs can also be added for extra flavour.

Potato bake

PHYLLIS HINGSTON, SASSAFRAS/WESLEY VALE BRANCH, TAS.

- 1 kg potatoes, peeled and thinly sliced
- 1 × 375-ml can evaporated milk
- pinch of nutmeg
- salt and pepper
- ½ cup grated cheese
- 60 g butter, chopped

SERVES 6–8

Preheat the oven to 180°C. Grease a shallow ovenproof dish with plenty of butter.

Layer potato slices in the prepared dish, then pour in evaporated milk, sprinkle with nutmeg and season with salt and pepper to taste. Scatter cheese over the top and dot with butter. Bake until top is golden and potatoes are tender (45–50 minutes).

Salmon patties

Delicious served with chips and salad or vegetables.

JULIE CHAPPEL, MILLOO BRANCH, VIC.

1 × 415-g can salmon
1½ cups cooked rice
2 dessertspoons vinegar
½ cup plain flour
salt and pepper
1 egg, beaten
breadcrumbs
oil or butter, for frying

MAKES 8

Put salmon in a bowl and mash with a fork, then combine with rice, vinegar, flour and seasonings. Roll mixture into balls, then flatten slightly. Dip patties in egg then coat with breadcrumbs. Fry in a little oil or butter until warmed through and golden.

Meat pasties or pies

HELEN WALL, CANIAMBO BRANCH, VIC.

1 onion, finely diced
1 stick celery, diced
oil
250 g beef mince
1 rasher bacon
chopped fresh parsley, to taste
1–3 cloves garlic, crushed
salt and pepper
ground nutmeg, to taste
1 bay leaf
1 strip lemon zest
1 cup tomato soup
1 × packet flaky or rough puff pastry
1 egg, beaten

MAKES 4

Preheat the oven to 200°C. Grease baking trays.

Fry the onion and celery in a little oil until transparent. Add the meat and fry until browned, breaking it up with a wooden spoon. Add remaining ingredients (except pastry and egg), and simmer gently until cooked (about 45 minutes – but the longer the better). Remove bay leaf and lemon zest.

To make pasties, cut pastry into rounds, wet the edge along one half of the round with water, then place a small amount of meat mixture in the centre. Fold pastry over and press edges together to seal, being careful not to flatten the filling. Place on prepared trays and brush with beaten egg.

To make pies, use pastry to line greased pie tins, fill with meat mixture, then cover each with a round of pastry and press around the edge to seal. Brush with beaten egg.

Bake pasties or pies in the oven until crisp and golden.

Potato critters

This is a good family meal for small children.

PHYLLIS HINGSTON, SASSAFRAS/WESLEY VALE BRANCH, TAS.

3 medium-sized potatoes
1 small onion
1 rounded tablespoon plain flour
chopped fresh parsley, to taste
salt and pepper
1 egg, beaten
oil for frying

SERVES 6–8

Grate potatoes and onion into a bowl. Add flour, parsley, and salt and pepper to taste. Mix in the beaten egg.

Heat a thin layer of oil in a frying pan. Drop tablespoons of mixture into the pan and cook until brown, then turn and brown the other side. Lower the heat and cook until potato is cooked through.

These are nice dipped in tomato sauce.

Cheese and chicken rissoles

This recipe came from my dear Auntie Vi in Melbourne, around 1970. It is really liked by everyone I make it for. Serve with a tossed salad and a nice glass of white wine.

WENDY WHITE, DARWIN BRANCH, NT

500 g lean chicken mince

½ onion, chopped very finely or grated

1 egg, beaten

2 tablespoons dry breadcrumbs

80 g fat-reduced tasty cheese, cut into 8 cubes

oil spray

MAKES 8

Mix together the mince, onion, egg and breadcrumbs. Shape mixture into eight balls. Press a cube of cheese into the centre of each and smooth the meat over to cover it completely. Lightly press each rissole to flatten slightly.

Spray a frying pan with oil and place over medium heat. Cook the rissoles for about 5 minutes on each side, or until cooked through.

Savoury toast and rat bait

We had Mum make this for all our parties when we lived in South Australia. Since moving to the Northern Territory, I've had to make it for all my South Australian friends who live in Darwin. At different times I have added extra ingredients like pineapple, mushrooms and olives. ('Rat bait' is what our family calls cheese.)

KAYLENE CONLAN, PORT DARWIN BRANCH, NT

1 cup tasty cheese, grated
2 eggs, well beaten
1 dessertspoon Worcestershire sauce
pinch of salt
pinch of cayenne pepper
4 rashers bacon, chopped
8 slices bread, buttered

SERVES 4

Preheat the oven to 200°C.

Mix together the cheese, eggs, sauce, salt, pepper and chopped bacon. Spread mixture on the buttered bread.

Place on baking trays and bake in the preheated oven for 15–20 minutes, or until crisp.

Potato and rocket salad

AILSA BOND A.M., RIVERSIDE BRANCH, TAS.

1 kg potatoes, cut in half
100 g rocket, chopped
1 red onion, finely sliced
1 teaspoon grated lemon zest

dressing

4 cloves garlic, unpeeled
2 tablespoons olive oil
2 tablespoons white vinegar
sugar, to taste
salt and pepper

SERVES 8

Preheat the oven to 180°C.

To make the dressing, wrap the garlic cloves in aluminium foil and bake in the oven for about 40 minutes. Cool, then remove skins and chop flesh. Combine garlic with the oil, vinegar, sugar, salt and pepper in a screw-top jar.

Boil the potatoes until tender (about 8 minutes). Drain.

Gently toss the potatoes with the rocket, onion, lemon zest and dressing, and serve.

Potato cakes

These potato cakes are delicious served with bacon or sausages – cooked tomato is also very nice.

JULIE CHAPPEL, MILLOO BRANCH, VIC.

3 or 4 large potatoes
1½ cups plain flour
1 teaspoon baking powder
1 egg
salt and pepper
oil or butter, for frying

MAKES 6

Boil potatoes until soft (about 20 minutes), then strain and mash. Combine with remaining ingredients and mix well. Shape into patties and fry in oil or butter until golden and cooked.

Cold chicken and rice salad

MRS. ARLENE ROBERTS, MOUNT MORGAN BRANCH, QLD

- 3 cups cooked chicken cut into strips
- 2 cups cooked rice (I use brown rice)
- ½ cup diced celery (optional)
- ¾ cup pineapple pieces
- ½ cup deep-fried almonds, chopped

dressing

- 3 tablespoons oil
- 2 teaspoons honey
- 1 teaspoon salt
- 1 teaspoon ground pepper
- good pinch of paprika
- 1 teaspoon curry powder
- ½ teaspoon cayenne pepper
- ½ teaspoon mixed herbs
- 2 tablespoons pineapple juice
- 2 dessertspoons lemon juice
- 2 tablespoons vinegar

SERVES 3–4

Place chicken in a bowl with the rice, celery and pineapple.

In a screw-top jar, combine all the dressing ingredients and shake well.

Pour the dressing over the salad and toss to combine. Scatter with the deep-fried almonds to serve.

Mains

Spaghetti pie

I created this recipe using leftovers from a normal spaghetti bolognese. My family has never been a big fan of lasagne, so this is our version.

MELISSA ANICTOMATIS, PORT DARWIN BRANCH, NT

1 × 500-g packet vermicelli spaghetti

1 egg, plus 1 egg yolk

mince mixture

1 teaspoon olive oil

1 onion, chopped

1 kg beef mince

2 cloves garlic, crushed

1 × 400-g can chopped tomatoes

700 ml passata

1 teaspoon Tuscan seasoning

1 teaspoon dried oregano

salt and cracked black pepper

1 teaspoon sugar

1 teaspoon balsamic vinegar

white sauce

60 g butter

3 teaspoons flour

1.5 litres milk

1 teaspoon mustard powder

salt and white pepper

200 g grated tasty cheese

100 g grated Romano cheese, plus extra for sprinkling

SERVES 6

Preheat the oven to 175°C.

To make the mince mixture, heat olive oil in a large pan and fry the onion until soft. Add mince and stir until well browned and separated. Add all other ingredients, along with 500 ml water and bring to the boil. Simmer until thickened (approximately 30 minutes).

To make the white sauce, melt the butter in a saucepan, add flour and cook briefly, stirring. Add the milk and mustard powder, salt and pepper, and cook over low heat until thickened, whisking continuously. Add grated cheeses and whisk until melted into the sauce.

Cook the pasta following directions on the packet. Drain, then mix with half of the white sauce. Whisk the egg and egg yolk into the remaining white sauce.

Pour the mince mixture into a large baking dish and spread the spaghetti mix on top. Pour the white sauce and egg mixture on top and sprinkle with the extra Romano cheese.

Bake in the oven until heated through and the top is lightly browned.

(Note: This is the basic recipe – chopped veggies of your liking can be added to the mince mixture to make this a real one-pot meal.)

Fish finger pie

This recipe was given to me by my cousin. Her mother would make it for the family when times were tough. My family loves it so much they often ask for Fish Finger Pie.

KARINA ZANCHETTA, GEORGE TOWN BRANCH, TAS.

- 2 kg potatoes, peeled and cut into small pieces
- 1 × 1-kg packet fish fingers (40 fingers in the packet)
- 1 × 600-g packet shredded cheese (I usually use tasty, but mozzarella works too)

SERVES 7–8

Preheat the oven to 180°C.

Put potatoes in a pot and cover with cold water. Bring to the boil and simmer for 20 minutes, until tender. Drain and mash.

Cook the fish fingers, or leave them frozen, as desired. In a casserole dish, arrange layers of fish fingers, shredded cheese (as much or as little as you like) and mashed potato, ending with a layer of potato followed by a generous layer of shredded cheese. Bake in the oven for 10–15 minutes, until hot through and cheese is melted.

(For variety, layers can also include cooked vegetables.)

Moussaka

NOELA MACLEOD, ESSENDON BRANCH, VIC.

- ½ cup olive oil
- 250 g zucchini, sliced
- 250 g eggplant, sliced
- 250 g potatoes, sliced
- 500 g beef mince
- 1 large onion, diced
- 1 clove garlic, finely chopped
- 2 tablespoons butter or margarine
- 1 tablespoon chopped fresh parsley
- 3 tomatoes, peeled and chopped (or 1 × 400-g can tomatoes)
- salt and pepper

béchamel sauce

- 45 g butter
- 45 g plain flour
- salt and pepper
- 2½ cups milk
- 1 bouquet garni
- ½ carrot, diced
- ½ turnip, diced
- ½ small onion, diced
- 1 stick celery, diced
- 1 tablespoon cream
- 1 egg
- ½ cup grated parmesan cheese, plus extra for the top

SERVES 4–6

Preheat the oven to 180°C. Grease a large baking dish.

Heat the oil in a large pan and fry the sliced vegetables until lightly browned.

In a separate frying pan, sauté mince, onion and garlic in the butter until meat is browned, then add the parsley, tomatoes, and salt and pepper. Cover and cook over a low heat for 20–30 minutes.

To make the béchamel sauce, place the butter, flour and seasonings in a saucepan and cook for a few minutes (do not let the mixture colour). Add the milk slowly, mixing well to avoid lumps. Add the bouquet garni and vegetables and stir until boiling. Simmer gently, preferably in a double boiler, for about 45 minutes. Remove bouquet garni, strain the sauce and check seasoning. Add the cream and reheat the sauce. Stir in the egg and the grated cheese.

Layer the cooked vegetables and meat mixture in the prepared baking dish. Spread the top with the béchamel sauce and scatter with some grated cheese. Bake in preheated oven until golden-brown (30–40 minutes).

(You can use fresh or dried herbs for the bouquet garni. You can buy small sachets of dried herbs, or make your own. The essential ingredient is parsley, including stalks and leaves if using fresh. I also include a bay leaf, a sprig of thyme, some marjoram and a small stalk of celery. If using fresh ingredients, tie with string; if using dried, place them in a muslin bag.)

Cheese savoury

ANITA MORRISH, VICTORIA HILL BRANCH, QLD

base

1 cup self-raising flour

55 g butter or margarine

¼ teaspoon salt

¼ teaspoon cayenne pepper

a good ½ cup grated Kraft processed cheddar cheese

topping

55 g butter or margarine

2 dessertspoons plain flour

1 cup milk

1 small onion, grated

chopped fresh parsley, to taste

¼ teaspoon salt

¼ teaspoon cayenne pepper

¾ cup grated cheese

1 egg, separated

SERVES 4

Preheat the oven to 180°C. Grease a Swiss roll tin.

To make the base, combine all ingredients with enough cold water to make a dough. Roll out dough and press into prepared tin.

Make a white sauce by combining all topping ingredients in a saucepan (except egg white), stirring over medium heat until thick and smooth. Beat the egg white until stiff peaks form and fold in.

Pour topping over the uncooked base and bake for about 30 minutes.

Hash of leftovers

This is a good way to use up leftover cold meat, and is a flexible dish that you can vary according to your taste (for example, you can substitute different vegetables for the carrots).

PATRICIA WALKER, GEORGE TOWN BRANCH, TAS.

12 medium-sized potatoes, peeled and sliced

3 medium-sized (or 2 large) onions, sliced

6 medium-sized carrots (or use other vegetables), thinly sliced

enough sliced leftover cold meat to make two or three layers

homemade chutney or relish (or use tomato sauce)

butter or shredded cheese, for topping

SERVES 6–8

Preheat the oven to 180°C. Lightly grease a rectangular oven dish (about 25-cm × 35-cm and 5-cm deep).

Place a layer of potato slices in the oven dish, followed by a layer of onions and then a layer of vegetables. Add a layer of meat and cover with chutney or relish. Repeat these layers until the dish is full (this may mean two or three layers, depending on how thick you make them). Finish with a layer of potato and top with small cubes of butter or shredded cheese.

Bake in the oven until the top layer of potato slices is cooked (30–45 minutes, depending on your oven).

Tangy sweet curry

NOLA TRELOAR, DEVONPORT BRANCH, TAS.

500 g lean steak, cubed
seasoned flour, to coat
2 medium-sized carrots, diced
1 large onion, chopped
2 sticks celery, diced
1 × 250-ml can tomato soup
1 small dessertspoon curry powder
1 tablespoon golden syrup
¼ cup lemon juice
salt and freshly ground black pepper

SERVES 4

Preheat the oven to 150°C (fan-forced).

Toss the steak in seasoned flour to coat, then place in a large casserole dish. Add carrot, onion and celery to the meat.

Mix the tomato soup with 1 cup water, then stir in the curry powder, golden syrup and lemon juice, and season with salt and pepper to taste. Add mixture to the meat and vegetables, stirring gently to combine. Place in oven and simmer for 2–3 hours.

Serve with steamed rice or mashed potato and peas.

Chicken pie

ELAINE YOUD, DEVONPORT BRANCH, TAS.

4 button mushrooms, sliced
1 medium-sized onion, sliced
⅓ cup oil
2 tablespoons plain flour
2 cups chicken stock
500 g cooked chicken, shredded
1 sprig fresh parsley
2 sheets puff pastry
1 beaten egg, mixed with a splash of milk

SERVES 4–6

Preheat the oven to 190°C. Grease a 25-cm pie plate.

Sauté mushrooms and onion in the oil until softened. Add flour and stir to combine, then pour in chicken stock. Simmer until thickened then add the cooked chicken and parsley.

Cut two rounds of pastry, big enough to fit the pie plate. Place one round onto the pie plate, pile chicken mixture on top, then paint around the edge of the pastry with the egg wash. Place the second round of pastry on top and press down around the edges to seal. Brush all over with egg wash. Bake until the pastry is golden-brown (20–25 minutes).

Rosy spare ribs

DULCIE FRENCH, CENTRAL COAST BRANCH, TAS.

2 tablespoons vinegar
4 tablespoons tomato sauce
dash of Worcestershire sauce
2 level tablespoons honey
12 pork spare ribs
garlic salt, to taste

SERVES 4–6

Preheat the oven to 180°C.

Combine vinegar, sauces and honey to make a marinade.

Sprinkle the ribs with garlic salt, then place on a wire rack set over a dish of water and bake for 25 minutes, turning once. (Alternatively you can cook them in a frying pan.) During the last 10 minutes of cooking, brush ribs with marinade frequently.

Macaroni special

You can multiply this recipe several times, then place in a large baking dish, sprinkle with grated cheese and cook in a hot oven until the cheese is melted – it serves up similar to lasagne and is very popular with large groups.

CARMA STUDLEY, METROPOLITAN BRANCH, TAS.

oil

700 g beef mince

1 medium-sized onion, diced

1 × 800-g can tomatoes or 1 × 550-g jar pasta sauce

1 × 500-g packet frozen mixed vegetables

salt and pepper

225 g elbow macaroni

225 g grated cheese

SERVES 6–8

Heat a little oil in a large pan, add meat and onion and cook until meat is browned, stirring frequently. Stir in tomatoes (with their liquid) or pasta sauce, 1 cup water and add all the remaining ingredients (except cheese). Bring to the boil, then reduce to a simmer and cook for about 20 minutes, until macaroni is tender – stir in the cheese about 10 minutes before the end of the cooking time. (Alternatively, you can simmer it for 15 minutes, then transfer to a casserole dish, sprinkle the cheese on top and bake in a moderate oven for about 20 minutes, until the cheese has melted and is starting to brown.)

Rich curry sauce with sausages

You can add desiccated coconut and sultanas to the sauce if desired.

HELEN WALL, CANIAMBO BRANCH, VIC.

8 sausages
1 tablespoon oil
½ onion, chopped
½ banana, chopped
1 tomato, chopped
½ apple, chopped
2 tablespoons plain flour
1 tablespoon curry powder
1 litre stock
2 tablespoons sugar
1 tablespoon chutney
1 tablespoon tomato sauce
1 tablespoon tomato paste
1 tablespoon redcurrant jelly
salt and pepper

SERVES 4

Cook the sausages in a large frying pan until done, then set aside.

In the same pan, heat the oil and fry the vegetables and fruit until browned. Add flour and curry powder and cook until browned. Add stock and remaining ingredients and stir until boiling, then reduce heat and simmer for 30 minutes.

Cut cooked sausages into pieces or leave whole, as desired, and add to the sauce. Simmer until warmed through.

Savoury leek pie

ELAINE YOUD, DEVONPORT BRANCH, TAS.

600 ml cream

200 g diced bacon

1 large onion, diced

1 × 60-g packet Continental Savoury Chicken Supreme soup mix

½ sweet potato, sliced

2–3 leeks, sliced

SERVES 4–6

Preheat the oven to 160°C.

Mix together cream, bacon, onion and soup mix. Place sweet potato and leeks in a casserole dish, pour cream mixture over, and bake in preheated oven until potatoes are cooked (20–30 minutes).

Beef and tomato mornay

NOELA MACLEOD, ESSENDON BRANCH, VIC.

1 dessertspoon butter
1 onion, finely chopped
500 g beef mince
125 g shredded cheese
1 × 820-g can tomato soup
salt and pepper
250 g macaroni or spaghetti
breadcrumbs, for topping

SERVES 4–6

Preheat the oven to 180°C. Grease a casserole dish.

Heat the butter in a frying pan and cook the onion until soft. Add the meat and brown well. Stir in half the cheese, the tomato soup, 1 cup water, and season with salt and pepper. Bring to the boil and add the pasta. Cover and simmer for 30 minutes, stirring occasionally. Place mixture into a casserole dish and sprinkle with remaining cheese and breadcrumbs. Bake until light-brown on top (about 30 minutes).

Tuna and potato casserole

This has been a favourite in our family for three generations.

JULIE CHAPPEL, MILLOO BRANCH, VIC.

1 × 425-g can tuna in brine
milk
60 g butter
3 tablespoons plain flour
¼ teaspoon salt
pepper
4 large potatoes, cooked and roughly chopped

topping

⅓ cup cream
¼ cup sugar
3 tablespoons vinegar
¾ teaspoon mustard powder
2 teaspoons Worcestershire sauce
½ cup grated cheese (more if preferred)

SERVES 6

Preheat the oven to 180°C. Grease a medium-sized casserole dish.

Drain tuna (reserving brine) and flake. Add enough milk to the brine to make up to 2 cups.

Melt butter in a large saucepan, then take off heat and blend in flour and seasonings. Return to heat and gradually add milk mixture, cooking until thick and smooth, while stirring constantly. Add tuna and mix well.

Arrange a layer of chopped potato in the casserole dish, then a layer of tuna mix. Repeat layers until all ingredients are used.

To make the topping, mix all ingredients together then spoon mixture over the tuna and potatoes. Bake in the preheated oven for about 30 minutes.

Fish in curry sauce

NOLA TRELOAR, DEVONPORT BRANCH, TAS.

2 tablespoons cooking oil

2 onions, finely chopped

2 cloves garlic, crushed

2 teaspoons curry powder

1 tablespoon tomato paste mixed with ¾ cup water

salt and freshly ground black pepper

4 fillets boneless fish

SERVES 4

Heat oil in a pan and fry the onion and garlic until tender. Add curry powder, stir over heat for a few minutes, then stir in tomato paste and water. Season to taste with salt and pepper.

Slide fish into the sauce and simmer gently until fish is cooked, stirring occasionally.

Serve with steamed white rice or mashed potato and pumpkin.

Bacon and egg pie

MRS. ARLENE ROBERTS, MOUNT MORGAN BRANCH, QLD

- 1 kg bacon rashers
- 4 eggs (or more if desired)
- 2–3 onions, sliced
- 2–3 tomatoes, sliced
- grated cheese, to scatter over the top

SERVES 4

Preheat the oven to 160°C. Grease a casserole or pie dish.

Arrange a layer of bacon rashers over the base of the prepared dish. Crack eggs on top of the bacon, then arrange a layer of onion slices on top, followed by a layer of tomato, another layer of bacon and more eggs if desired. Repeat these layers until the dish is nearly full. Bake in the oven for 30–45 minutes, until cooked. (When there's about 10 minutes to go, scatter grated cheese over the top.)

Serve with cooked vegetables or salad.

Asparagus chicken casserole

L.C. JONES, DEVONPORT BRANCH, TAS.

- ½ cup oil
- 750 g chicken pieces
- 1 onion, sliced
- 125 g bacon, chopped
- ¼ cup plain flour
- 1 cup milk
- 1 × 440-g can asparagus cuts
- 2 chicken stock cubes
- 1 tablespoon lemon juice
- salt and pepper
- 90 g cheddar cheese
- 2 tablespoons chopped fresh parsley, to serve

SERVES 6

Preheat the oven to 180°C.

Heat oil in a frying pan, add chicken pieces and cook, turning occasionally, until well browned. Transfer chicken to an ovenproof dish and set aside.

Add onion and bacon to the pan and sauté until onion is transparent. Stir in the flour, then remove pan from heat and add milk, 1 cup water, asparagus (undrained), crumbled stock cubes, lemon juice, and salt and pepper. Stir until mixture is combined, then return to the stove. Bring to the boil, stirring, and simmer until sauce thickens. Stir in the cheese.

Pour sauce over the chicken pieces and bake, covered, for 45–55 minutes.

Garnish with parsley before serving.

Impossible quiche

ELAINE YOUD, DEVONPORT BRANCH, TAS.

1 cup grated cheese
½ cup self-raising flour
1 onion, chopped
4 eggs, beaten
1½ cups milk
200 g diced bacon
1 tablespoon chopped fresh parsley
salt and pepper

SERVES 4–6

Preheat oven to 175°C. Grease a 25-cm round pie dish.

Stir all the ingredients together and season with salt and pepper. Place in prepared dish and bake for 20 minutes.

Spaghetti with minced steak

HELEN WALL, CANIAMBO BRANCH, VIC.

knob of butter

2 rashers bacon, cut into squares

1 medium-sized onion, chopped

500 g minced steak

½ × 500-g packet spaghetti (or spirals, penne or other pasta of your choice)

1 × 850-g can tomato soup

grated cheese, to serve

SERVES 4–6

Heat butter in a pan, add the bacon and onion and cook until browned. Add mince, and cook until browned.

Meanwhile, cook the pasta in salted boiling water until just tender. Drain.

Add cooked spaghetti to the meat mixture, pour in tomato soup, and mix well until combined and heated through.

Serve scattered with grated cheese.

Onion marinated beef

JANET AVERY, LATROBE BRANCH, TAS.

- 1 kg round steak, in one piece
- ½ × 40-g packet French Onion soup mix
- ⅔ cup tomato juice
- 1 teaspoon freshly squeezed lemon juice
- salt and pepper
- 3 medium-sized onions, thinly sliced
- 1 clove garlic, crushed
- 1 tablespoon oil
- 3 medium-sized tomatoes, peeled and chopped
- 2 teaspoons fresh oregano (or 1 teaspoon dried)
- 2 teaspoons chopped fresh parsley

SERVES 6

Preheat grill or barbecue.

Snip the fat surrounding the steak in three or four places. Blend together the soup powder, tomato juice and lemon juice. Season with salt and pepper to taste and rub into the steak. Prick meat all over with a skewer, place on a dish and set aside to marinate for 10 minutes.

Fry onion and garlic in oil until onion is soft. Add tomatoes, oregano and parsley, then drain the marinade liquid from the meat into the pan and bring to the boil. Keep sauce hot while you grill or barbecue the steak for about 6 minutes on each side, until done to your liking. Place on a serving dish and pour the hot sauce over. Cut into portions before serving.

Seafood casserole

DULCIE FRENCH, CENTRAL COAST BRANCH, TAS.

- 1 apple, chopped
- 1 onion, chopped
- ½ cup chopped celery
- 2 tablespoons butter
- 1 × 70-g packet Continental Dutch Curry and Rice soup mix
- 1 × 425-g can tuna, drained
- 3 teaspoons lemon juice
- salt and pepper
- 1 dessertspoon sultanas

SERVES 4–6

Preheat the oven to 180°C. Grease a casserole dish.

Fry apple, onion and celery in the butter until soft. Add the soup mix and stir well, then gradually blend in 475 ml water. Cover pan and simmer for 15 minutes, stirring regularly.

Add tuna, lemon juice, a pinch of salt and pepper, and the sultanas to the pan. Mix thoroughly, transfer to prepared casserole dish, cover and bake until heated thoroughly (about 1 hour).

Serve with potatoes or crusty bread.

Porcupine meatballs

This recipe is a favourite with kids.

MRS. ANNETTE FERGUSSON, ORIELTON BRANCH, TAS.

500 g beef mince
½ cup rice
1 onion, finely chopped
1 carrot, grated
1 stick celery, thinly sliced
1 teaspoon salt (optional)
3 shakes of pepper
1 × 425-g can tomato soup

SERVES 4–8

Preheat oven or electric frying pan to 200°C. Grease a casserole dish with butter (if using oven).

Put the beef, rice, onion, carrot, celery, salt and pepper in a bowl. Using your hands, combine well, then shape mixture into small balls. Place the meatballs in prepared casserole dish or frying pan. Mix tomato soup with 1 cup water in the same bowl the meat was mixed in, and pour this liquid over the meatballs. Cover and cook for 1 hour.

Serve with mashed potatoes and/or green vegetables.

Kedgeree

As one gets older, quick and easy recipes are the way to go. This is a family favourite, especially with my grandchildren.

L. C. JONES, DEVONPORT BRANCH, TAS.

4 tablespoons long-grain rice
1 cup milk
60 g butter, melted
1 dessertspoon cornflour
1 teaspoon curry powder
1 × 210-g can salmon
2 hardboiled eggs, chopped
salt
chopped fresh parsley, for garnish

SERVES 4

Cook the rice in salted boiling water for 20 minutes, then drain.

Heat milk and butter in a large saucepan and when butter is just melting, add the cornflour and curry powder. Stir over low heat until the mixture thickens, then add cooked rice, salmon and eggs. Stir until well combined, adding salt to taste.

Serve hot, garnished with parsley.

Rebecca's leek and sweet potato pie

This is my daughter's pie recipe. Yum.

ELAINE YOUD, DEVONPORT BRANCH, TAS.

pastry

90 g butter

2½ tablespoons milk

1 cup self-raising flour

filling

2–3 medium-sized leeks

125 g bacon pieces

2 tablespoons butter

½ medium-sized sweet potato, chopped

1 × 125-g can corn kernels

4 eggs

½ cup milk

1 cup grated cheese

SERVES 6

Preheat the oven to 190°C. Grease a 25-cm pie plate.

To make the pastry, melt butter and milk in a saucepan, then add sifted flour and mix to combine. Roll dough into a ball, then press into the pie plate.

Sauté leek and bacon in a pan with the butter until softened. Meanwhile, parboil the sweet potato. Drain. Place all the vegetables into the pastry case.

Beat together the eggs, milk and cheese, then pour mixture over the vegetables. Bake in the preheated oven for 20 minutes, then reduce temperature to 180°C and bake for another 20 minutes.

T-bones in the oven

JUDY ANICTOMATIS, DARWIN BRANCH, NT

4 T-bone steaks
2 cloves garlic, thinly sliced
375 g canned chopped tomatoes
1 tablespoon tomato paste
1 tablespoon butter
salt and pepper

SERVES 4

Preheat the oven to 150°C.

Place steaks in a baking dish and sprinkle with garlic. Pour in the canned tomatoes.

Stir the tomato paste into 2 cups water and add to dish. Dot the steaks with knobs of butter, and season with salt and pepper. Bake in the preheated oven for 2 hours, basting the steaks with the pan juices occasionally. (If it becomes too dry during cooking, just add more water.)

Serve with some creamy mashed potato and steamed vegetables.

Tuna casserole

NOELA MACLEOD, ESSENDON BRANCH, VIC.

8 cups cooked rice
1 × 425-g tin tuna, drained
corn-flake crumbs, for topping
butter, for dotting

cheese sauce

3 dessertspoons butter
3 dessertspoons plain flour
salt and pepper
½ teaspoon curry powder
2½ cups milk
185 g grated cheese

SERVES 4

Preheat the oven to 200°C. Grease a casserole dish.

To make the cheese sauce, melt the butter in a saucepan, then add the flour, salt, pepper and curry powder. Stir to combine. Gradually add the milk, stirring all time, and heat until thickened. Stir in the grated cheese.

Place alternate layers of cooked rice, tuna and cheese sauce in the prepared casserole dish. Cover with corn-flake crumbs and dot with butter. Bake until golden and bubbling (about 30 minutes).

Bobotie

My sister-in-law, Kay, gave me this recipe. She had this dish when she visited South Africa. Bobotie is traditionally made with meat left over from the Sunday roast.

WENDY WHITE, DARWIN BRANCH, NT

1 thick slice white bread
1 cup milk
1 kg beef mince (or use mutton)
1 onion, finely chopped
½ cup sultanas
½ cup blanched almonds
3 teaspoons smooth apricot jam
3 teaspoons fruit chutney
1 tablespoon lemon juice
1 teaspoon chopped fresh herbs
2 teaspoons curry powder
1 teaspoon turmeric
2 teaspoons salt
2 teaspoons sunflower oil
3 large eggs
4 bay leaves (or lemon leaves)

yellow rice
1 cup rice
½ cup sultanas
2 teaspoons turmeric
1 stick cinnamon
1½ tablespoons soft brown sugar
salt
knob of butter

SERVES 6

Preheat the oven to 180°C. Grease a casserole dish.

Soak the bread in ½ cup of the milk, then squeeze it dry – reserve the milk and add it to remaining ½ cup milk. Mix the bread with the meat and all other ingredients except the milk, oil, eggs and bay leaves.

Heat the oil in a frying pan and lightly brown the meat mixture. Transfer to the prepared casserole dish.

Beat the eggs with the remaining milk, then pour over the meat. Garnish the top with bay or lemon leaves and bake in the preheated oven for about 50 minutes, or until custard has set.

Make the yellow rice by cooking the rice in boiling water with all other ingredients (except butter), until tender (12–15 minutes). Drain and remove cinnamon stick, then stir in butter.

Serve bobotie with yellow rice on the side.

Vegetable quiche

You can use any vegetables you fancy in this quiche. In my version, I add all the veggies mentioned below. Happy eating, all.

HEATHER J. COOPER, DEVONPORT BRANCH, TAS.

1 cup grated cheese
1 onion, finely chopped
½ cup self-raising flour
4 eggs, beaten
1½ cups milk
salt and pepper
2 cups assorted chopped vegetables (tomato, zucchini, celery, capsicum, mushroom, carrot)

SERVES 6

Preheat the oven to 180°C. Grease a medium-sized round quiche dish.

Mix all the ingredients together and pour into the quiche dish. Cook for 45 minutes in the oven, or until eggs are cooked.

Carrot and lentil loaf

This is a very tasty dish.

CAROLINE JOSWIG, TENNANT CREEK BRANCH, NT

3 tablespoons olive oil
2 onions, chopped
2 carrots, finely grated
225 g red lentils
400 ml vegetable stock
2 tablespoons mango chutney
2 tablespoons tomato paste
200 g almonds, chopped
2 eggs, lightly beaten

filling

100 g mature tasty cheddar cheese, grated
1 cup fresh white breadcrumbs
juice of 2 lemons
½ cup finely chopped fresh parsley

sauce

2 × 450-g cans chopped tomatoes
a few drops Tabasco sauce
1 tablespoon vinegar
1 teaspoon sugar
salt and pepper

SERVES 6

Preheat the oven to 200°C. Line the base and sides of a 400-ml loaf tin with baking paper.

Heat oil in a pan and cook onions for about 5 minutes, until softened. Stir in the carrot and cook for a further 4 minutes, then add the lentils and stock. Bring to the boil and simmer until lentils are cooked (about 25 minutes), stirring occasionally and adding more stock if necessary. Leave to cool.

Once cooled, add the chutney, tomato paste, almonds and eggs to the lentils. Spoon two-thirds of this mixture into the loaf tin, making sure the mixture covers the base and sides of the tin.

To make the filling, mix together the cheese, breadcrumbs, lemon juice and chopped parsley. Spoon mixture into the loaf tin, then spread the remaining lentils on top. Cover with aluminium foil and bake for 1 hour and 20 minutes.

While the loaf is cooking, make the tomato sauce. Blend all the ingredients in a blender, then pour into a saucepan, bring to the boil and simmer for 20 minutes.

Serve the loaf sliced, with the sauce spooned over.

Citrus chicken breasts

LORNA JONES, DEVONPORT BRANCH, TAS.

90 g butter
4 chicken breasts, each cut in half
½ cup white wine
grated zest of 1 orange
grated zest of 1 lemon
salt and pepper
¾ cup cream
90 g grated cheese

SERVES 8

Preheat grill to medium.

Heat butter in a large frying pan, add chicken breasts and brown on both sides. Reduce heat, cover pan and cook for 15 minutes, turning several times, until cooked through. Transfer chicken to a shallow heatproof serving dish and keep warm.

Add wine to the frying pan and stir for a few minutes. Add orange and lemon zests, and season with salt and pepper to taste. Increase heat and slowly stir in cream. When thoroughly combined, pour sauce over the chicken and sprinkle with grated cheese. Place under the grill to brown the cheese.

Pot roast of topside

BEV LITTLEJOHN, MIRBOO BRANCH, VIC.

1 tablespoon oil
1–1.5 kg beef topside, in one piece
¼ cup soy sauce
¼ cup soft brown sugar
cornflour (if needed)

SERVES 4–6

Heat the oil in a heavy-based saucepan and brown the meat on all sides.

Blend the soy sauce and sugar with ½ cup water until sugar is dissolved. Pour this mixture over the beef, cover the saucepan and simmer very gently for about 2 hours, until meat is tender. (You can thicken the gravy with a little cornflour if needed.)

Salmon and pineapple casserole

NOELA MACLEOD, ESSENDON BRANCH, VIC.

100 g butter

⅓ cup plain flour

pinch of salt

cayenne pepper, to taste

2 cups milk

1 × 415-g can salmon, drained

1 × 450-g can crushed pineapple, drained

50 g corn flakes

SERVES 4–6

Preheat the oven to 180°C. Grease a casserole dish.

Melt half the butter in a saucepan and add the flour, salt and cayenne pepper to taste, stirring to form a roux. Gradually add the milk and let the sauce thicken, stirring all the time. Stir in the tin of salmon.

Place a layer of the mixture into the prepared casserole dish, then add a layer of the crushed pineapple. Continue layering, finishing with the salmon mixture. Melt the remaining butter in a saucepan, add the corn flakes and toss to coat. Scatter corn-flake mixture over the top of the casserole. Cook in the oven until golden-brown (about 20 minutes).

Colo's curry pie

Colo is short for Coleman, which is my parents' surname.

SHIRLEY PLATZ, MIDDLE RIDGE BRANCH, QLD

2 tablespoons oil
1 kg stewing steak, cut into pieces
2 onions, chopped
1 clove garlic, crushed
grated ginger, to taste (optional)
1 cooking apple, peeled, cored and chopped
1 cup sliced celery
1 cup sliced carrot
1 × 400-g can whole peeled tomatoes
1 tablespoon sugar
1 tablespoon curry powder
salt and pepper
½ cup sultanas
2 cups cooked rice
1 cup grated cheese
1 cup barbecue-flavour chips, crushed

SERVES 8

Heat oil in a frying pan and brown meat in batches. Remove meat from pan and set aside. Tip the onion, garlic and ginger into the pan and cook until onions are soft. Return meat to the pan and add the apple, vegetables, seasonings and sultanas. Simmer gently for 1½–2 hours.

Preheat the oven to 150°C.

Layer the meat mixture with the cooked rice in an ovenproof dish. Top with grated cheese and crushed chips and cook in the oven for 10 minutes, until heated through and cheese is melted.

All-in-one spaghetti

This quick and simple meal is very popular when my family comes for lunch on a weekend and they don't want to eat a roast or heavy meal. It is very nice served with garlic bread.

JUDY PRATT, DARWIN BRANCH, NT

1 dessertspoon cooking oil
1 large onion, chopped
250 g beef mince
1½ teaspoons salt
¼ teaspoon ground pepper
1 cup shredded cheese
1 × 425-g can tomato soup
100 g thin spaghetti

SERVES 4–6

Heat oil in a large pan and cook onion till soft. Add mince and cook until browned, then sprinkle with salt and pepper. Add half the cheese, the tomato soup and 1 cup water and bring to the boil. Add spaghetti a little at a time. Cover and simmer for 20–30 minutes over very low heat, stirring almost constantly so the cheese does not stick to the pan.

Tuna casserole with mushrooms

WILMA DELL, DEVONPORT BRANCH, TAS.

3 cups cooked rice

1 × 440-g can mushroom soup

1 × 250-g can tuna

salt and freshly ground black pepper

1 small onion, finely chopped

1 dessertspoon grainy mustard

¾ cup finely chopped celery

125 g grated cheese

fresh parsley and tomato wedges, to serve

SERVES 2–4

Preheat the oven to 180°C. Grease a casserole dish.

Combine all ingredients, reserving half the cheese. Mix well, then transfer to the prepared casserole dish. Sprinkle with the reserved cheese and bake for approximately 20 minutes.

Garnish with parsley and serve with tomato wedges on the side.

Beef rissoles and salad

MRS. ARLENE ROBERTS, MOUNT MORGAN BRANCH, QLD

rissoles

2 kg mince
1 large onion, finely chopped
1 large tomato, finely chopped
1 large carrot, finely grated
salt and pepper
plain flour
1 egg
cooking oil

salad

12–14 lettuce leaves
3 tomatoes, cut into wedges
1 red onion, sliced
1 cup grated or diced cheese
1 cup grated carrot
3 cups pineapple pieces
1 × 450-g can beetroot slices
3–4 cups potato salad

SERVES 6–8

To make the rissoles, place mince in a deep bowl, add onion and tomato along with carrot, and salt and pepper. Add a sprinkle of flour and mix thoroughly.

Make a well in the centre of the mixture, and crack in the egg. Mix again, to combine the egg with the other ingredients. Roll tablespoons of mixture into balls, then pat them flat and coat in a little flour. Fry rissoles in oil, cooking for 2–3 minutes on each side, until browned and cooked through.

For the salad, place two lettuce leaves on each plate, along with 2–3 wedges of tomato, 2–3 slices of onion, 2 dessertspoons cheese, 2 dessertspoons grated carrot, ½ cup pineapple, 2–3 slices beetroot and ½ cup potato salad. Serve rissoles alongside the salad.

Corn 'n' seafood bake

NOELA MACLEOD, ESSENDON BRANCH, VIC.

- 4 level tablespoons butter, plus extra for dotting
- 1 medium-sized onion, chopped
- 4 level tablespoons plain flour
- 2 cups milk
- ½ cup shredded cheese
- 1 cup cooked peas
- 1 × 425-g can tuna, drained and flaked
- salt and pepper
- 1 cup corn-flake crumbs
- chopped tomato and fresh parsley, for garnish
- lemon wedges, to serve

SERVES 4–5

Preheat oven to 180°C. Grease a casserole dish.

Melt the butter in a pan and fry the onion until soft but not browned. Add the flour and blend. Pour in the milk, stirring constantly. Bring to the boil and simmer for 2–3 minutes. Stir in the cheese, peas, tuna and seasoning to taste. Pour mixture into prepared casserole dish, cover with the corn-flake crumbs and dot with butter. Bake for 20 minutes in the oven.

Serve hot, garnished with tomato and parsley, with lemon wedges on the side.

Mushroom pie

CAROLINE JOSWIG, TENNANT CREEK BRANCH, NT

pastry

2 cups plain flour

125 g butter, chopped

filling

1½ tablespoons butter

6 spring onions, chopped

2 small cloves garlic, chopped

375 g mushrooms, sliced

1 teaspoon white or brown miso paste

½ cup cream

3 tablespoons cornflour

handful coriander leaves, chopped

3 cups mashed sweet potato

SERVES 4–6

Preheat the oven to 180°C. Grease a 20-cm pie dish.

To make the shortcrust pastry, sift the flour into a bowl, then work in the butter and a small amount of iced water, until it forms a dough. Roll out and use to line the prepared pie dish.

To make the filling, melt the butter in a pan and fry the spring onions and garlic for a couple of minutes until golden. Add mushrooms and fry gently until softened. Add miso and cream. Mix cornflour with 3 tablespoons water and add to the mushroom mixture. Cook gently for about 5 minutes, adding a little more water if necessary.

Stir coriander into the mashed sweet potato. Pour mushroom mixture into the pie shell, then cover with the mash. Bake in the oven for about 20 minutes, until pastry is cooked. Serve with a crisp green salad.

Mince and spaghetti (the easy way)

WILMA DELL, DEVONPORT BRANCH, TAS.

500 g beef mince (preferably fat-free mince)

oil

1 onion, finely chopped

1 × 420-g can spaghetti in tomato sauce

SERVES 2–4

Place mince in a saucepan with a little oil and cook until browned. Add onion and cook for 5 minutes, then pour off any liquid (especially if not using fat-free mince). Stir in the spaghetti and heat through.

Serve with mashed potatoes and vegetables if desired.

Chicken and soy sauce

This recipe is a favourite in our family. It was always called for when my children returned home for the holidays.

JUDY ANICTOMATIS, DARWIN BRANCH, NT

- 1 whole chicken, cut into 8 portions
- 100 ml soy sauce
- 200 ml light soy sauce
- 100 ml kecap manis (dark sweet soy sauce)
- 2½ tablespoons Worcestershire sauce
- 2½ tablespoons butter, chopped
- white pepper
- steamed white rice and grated Romano cheese, to serve

SERVES 4

Preheat the oven to 180°C.

Place chicken pieces, skin-side up, in a baking dish. Mix the soy sauces with the Worcestershire sauce and 100 ml water and pour over the chicken pieces. Place a knob of butter on each piece of chicken and sprinkle with white pepper. Bake for about 1 hour, or until chicken is cooked through and skin is crispy. (Baste once, about halfway through cooking time, and add more water if the pan becomes too dry.)

Serve chicken, with the sauce from the pan, over steamed white rice. Sprinkle with some grated Romano cheese.

Layer casserole

HELEN WALL, CANIAMBO BRANCH, VIC.

½ cup rice
500 g minced steak
1¼ cups chopped onion
¼ cup chopped green capsicum
½ cup sweet corn kernels
1 × 450-g can tomato soup
1 cup grated tasty cheese
2 rashers bacon
salt and pepper

SERVES 4–6

Preheat the oven to 180°C. Grease a casserole dish.

Spread the rice over the base of the prepared casserole dish. Cover with a layer of minced steak, followed by a layer of onion, green capsicum and sweet corn, seasoning with salt and pepper between each layer. Pour the tomato soup over and sprinkle with the grated tasty cheese. Place bacon rashers on top. Cook on the bottom shelf of the oven for 1½ hours.

French chicken casserole

MRS. ARLENE ROBERTS, MOUNT MORGAN BRANCH, QLD

2 whole chickens (size 14 or 16), cut into pieces
½–1 cup Worcestershire sauce
1 × 810-g can crushed tomatoes
1 × 40-g packet French Onion soup

SERVES 6

Preheat the oven to 220°C.

Place chicken pieces in a baking dish. Sprinkle Worcestershire sauce over all the chicken pieces, then pour tomatoes over. Now sprinkle soup mix over the top of the tomatoes. Pour over enough hot water to cover the chicken. Bake for 1½ hours or until chicken is cooked, turning chicken pieces after 45 minutes.

Serve with mashed veggies, peas and gravy.

Pizza dough

Our daughter Jayne, who lives in Canberra, gave me this recipe. I have passed it on to so many people as it is easy and wonderful fun to make. Children can organise their own toppings to make individual pizzas.

WENDY WHITE, DARWIN BRANCH, NT

¾ cup boiling water mixed with 1¼ cups cold water
2 teaspoons sugar
4 teaspoons dry yeast
3½–3¾ cups plain flour
1 teaspoon salt
2 tablespoons olive oil

MAKES 6 SMALL OR 2 LARGE PIZZAS

Pour a quarter of the lukewarm water into a bowl and add a pinch of the sugar, then whisk in the yeast until dissolved. Set aside for about 5 minutes until the mixture starts to bubble.

Meanwhile, sift the flour, salt and remaining sugar into a bowl and make a well in the centre.

Add remaining water and the oil to the yeast mixture, then pour it into the well in the flour. Use your hands or an electric mixer to mix until it forms a thick sticky paste – add some extra flour if the mixture is too runny, or some more water if it is too dry. Mix dough for about 2 minutes, then cover the bowl with a clean tea towel and leave in a warm place for about an hour, until it has doubled in size.

Preheat the oven to 190°C.

Put the dough on a work surface that has been dusted with flour and punch it down. Divide dough into two or more pieces (depending on the size of the pizzas you will be making). Shape portions into balls, then rest for another 10 minutes. Roll dough out to make pizza bases. Top with your favourite toppings and cook for about 20 minutes.

Suggested toppings

Kids' favourite: Tomato paste, grated cheese and ham.

Roasted vegetable: Tomato paste, mixed roasted vegetables, grated cheese and ham.

Caramelised onion: Caramelised onion and crumbled blue cheese (don't use tomato paste for this one).

My favourite: Tomato paste, grated cheese, ham or salami, mushrooms, olives, bocconcini slices, and a little grated mozzarella on top.

Basil: As above but with fresh basil leaves instead of the mushrooms.

My husband's favourite: Tomato paste, ham, mushrooms, cooked beef and grated cheese.

Tasmanian apple casserole

MARGARET FELDTMANN, DOOKIE BRANCH, VIC.

- 1 tablespoon olive oil
- 2 tablespoons plain flour
- 4 mutton forequarter chops, trimmed and cut into bite-size pieces
- 1 onion, sliced
- 1 green apple, diced
- 1½ cups apple juice
- salt and pepper
- ½ cup chopped fresh mint

SERVES 4

Preheat the oven to 180°C.

Heat oil in a pan, add flour and meat and cook until browned. Remove meat and set aside. Add onion and apple to the pan and cook until browned. Return meat to the pan, then pour in apple juice and bring to the boil. Season with salt and pepper and stir in the mint. Transfer to a casserole dish, cover and cook in the oven for 1–1½ hours.

Serve with mashed potatoes, green beans and carrots.

Meat loaf

DULCIE FRENCH, CENTRAL COAST BRANCH, TAS.

1 cup breadcrumbs

500 g beef mince

500 g sausage mince

2 medium-sized carrots, grated

1 onion, chopped

1 egg

tomato sauce and Worcestershire sauce, to taste

SERVES 6–8

Preheat the oven to 200°C. Lightly grease two loaf tins.

Combine all the ingredients in a bowl, mixing well. Divide mixture between the loaf tins. Bake in the preheated oven for about 40 minutes, until cooked through.

Sweet endings

Chocolate self-saucing pudding

MELISSA ANICTOMATIS, PORT DARWIN BRANCH, NT

⅓ cup soft brown sugar
1 cup self-raising flour
2 tablespoons cocoa
½ cup milk
60 g butter, melted and cooled
1 egg
thickened cream or vanilla ice-cream, to serve

sauce

⅔ cup soft brown sugar
¼ cup cocoa
1¼ cups boiling water

SERVES 4–6

Preheat the oven to 170°C. Grease a 1-litre ovenproof dish with butter.

Combine the sugar with the sifted flour and cocoa. Whisk together the milk, butter and egg. Add the dry ingredients to the wet ingredients and beat until smooth. Pour mixture into the prepared dish and use the back of a spoon to smooth the surface.

To make the sauce, combine the sugar and sifted cocoa and sprinkle it evenly over the pudding batter. Gradually and evenly pour the boiling water over the top.

Bake for 35–45 minutes or until a cake-like topping forms on the surface and a skewer inserted into the centre of the pudding comes out clean. Set aside to cool for about 5 minutes before serving warm with cream or ice-cream.

Orange cake

DULCIE FRENCH, CENTRAL COAST BRANCH, TAS.

180 g self-raising flour
180 g sugar
90 g softened butter
2 eggs
zest of 1 orange
juice of 1 orange (to make ½ cup – if necessary make up with milk)

SERVES 12–18

Preheat the oven to 180°C. Grease a 20-cm cake tin.

Beat all ingredients together until well combined. Pour mixture into prepared tin and bake for 30–40 minutes.

Smooth heaven

This recipe was given to me many years again by a dear lady at our church. She made this dessert for many of our church functions. I have made it many times since and always have the same result (everyone loves it).

KARINA ZANCHETTA, GEORGE TOWN BRANCH, TAS.

¾ cup orange juice
¾ cup pineapple juice
½ cup sugar
1 × 85-g packet lemon jelly crystals
1 × 375-ml can evaporated milk
juice of 1 lemon
fruit, to serve (optional)

SERVES 6–10

Heat fruit juices, sugar and jelly in a saucepan until sugar has dissolved. Pour into a bowl to cool. When beginning to set, whip well. In a separate bowl, whip evaporated milk until it's three times its original volume, then add lemon juice and jelly and whip again. Transfer to a serving dish. Serve with fruit if desired.

Madeira cake

TRISH JACOBSON, CHILDERS BRANCH, QLD

230 g softened butter
230 g sugar
1 tablespoon hot water
5 eggs
few drops lemon essence
285 g plain flour
1 teaspoon baking powder
pinch of salt

SERVES 8

Preheat the oven to 160°C. Grease a 20-cm cake tin.

Cream butter, sugar and hot water. Add eggs one at a time, beating well. Beat in lemon essence, then sifted flour, baking powder and salt. Pour into prepared tin and bake for approximately 1 hour.

Apple delight

This dish has proven very popular with hungry farm workers and also at progressive dinners. I've been asked for the recipe many times.

ALWYN HILLS, WYNYARD BRANCH, TAS.

1 cup self-raising flour
pinch of salt
1 tablespoon sugar
1 large apple, grated
½ cup milk
ground cinnamon, for sprinkling

sauce

1 cup soft brown sugar
2 tablespoons butter
2 cups boiling water

SERVES 6

Preheat the oven to 180°C. Grease a 21-cm × 16-cm casserole dish.

Sift flour and salt together, add sugar and apple and mix with milk to make a scone dough. Put into prepared baking dish.

To make the sauce, combine the sugar, butter and boiling water, stirring until sugar has dissolved and butter melted. Pour sauce over the scone mixture and sprinkle with cinnamon. Bake for 20–25 minutes. (When cooked it has a golden biscuit topping and a lovely tasty sauce underneath.)

Lemon pudding

EILEEN McMULLEN, RANELAGH BRANCH, TAS.

1 tablespoon softened butter
¾ cup sugar
2 tablespoons plain flour
juice and grated zest of 1 lemon
2 eggs, separated
1 cup milk
custard or cream, to serve

SERVES 6

Preheat the oven to 160°C. Grease a 20-cm baking dish.

Cream butter and sugar, add sifted flour, lemon juice and zest, along with the egg yolks and milk. Beat egg whites until soft peaks form, then fold into the lemon mixture. Pour into prepared dish and bake for 1 hour. Serve with custard or cream.

Pantomime cake

This cake is a favourite with my family for birthdays. For a quick and easy alternative, use a piece of bought cake instead of making the madeira cake from scratch. You can make the marshmallow any colour, but I think pink looks best. Green is great fun for St. Patrick's Day.

TRISH JACOBSON, CHILDERS BRANCH, QLD

½ a 3-day-old madeira cake (page 137), cut into cubes

1 × 125-g block chocolate (fruit and nut or plain), cut into small pieces

desiccated coconut, to coat

marshmallow

1 heaped tablespoon gelatine

1 cup hot water

2 cups sugar

food colouring

SERVES 12–20

To make the marshmallow, add gelatine to ½ cup of the hot water and stir to dissolve. Put sugar and remaining ½ cup hot water in a bowl, and stir to dissolve sugar. Add gelatine mixture and a few drops food colouring and beat for 10 minutes.

Mix together the cake pieces, chocolate and most of the marshmallow mixture, reserving about 1 cup of the marshmallow for topping. (Note that if you partially freeze the cake pieces first, they will not brake up as much when mixing.) Put mixture in a greased deep 20-cm round tin or mould and top with remaining marshmallow. Place in refrigerator overnight to set.

Sprinkle coconut over a sheet of baking paper and tip the cake out onto the paper, to coat the top with coconut. Carefully roll the sides of the cake in coconut. Place cake onto a serving plate and sprinkle more coconut on top if desired.

Crème caramel

MELISSA ANICTOMATIS, PORT DARWIN BRANCH, NT

caramel

1 cup sugar

custard

1 × 395-g can condensed milk

3 eggs, plus 3 egg yolks

2 teaspoons caster sugar

2 cups milk

1 teaspoon vanilla essence or the seeds from 1 vanilla bean

MAKES 1 LARGE OR 8 SMALL

Preheat the oven to 150°C.

To make the caramel, combine sugar with ½ cup water in a saucepan and simmer until light-caramel in colour. Pour into a 1-litre mould, or eight 125-ml ramekins. Leave to set and cool completely.

Whisk together all custard ingredients. Pass custard through a fine sieve into the mould/s.

Bake in a bain-marie (water bath) for 45 minutes, or until the custard is just set (it should still have a slight wobble in the centre). Let stand at room temperature until cool, then chill overnight (or for about 6 hours).

To serve, run a small knife around the edge of the custard to loosen, then carefully invert onto serving plates.

Healthy fruit cake

This cake has no butter, eggs or sugar, and is made with wholemeal flour. It keeps well and is very easy to make.

JANE BEAVAN, ROCHES BEACH BRANCH, TAS.

- 1 kg mixed dried fruit (you can add dates or any other dried fruit you like)
- orange juice (I don't measure, but about 2 cups)
- rum, brandy or sherry (optional)
- about 2 cups wholemeal self-raising flour (or plain self-raising flour if you prefer)

MAKES 1 LARGE CAKE OR 2–3 SMALLER ONES (SERVES 16–20)

Put the mixed fruit in a bowl and cover with orange juice. Add a splash of alcohol if desired. Leave to stand overnight.

Preheat the oven to 120–130°C. Grease a 20-cm square or round cake tin (or you can use two or three smaller ones).

Add enough sifted flour to the fruit mixture to take up all the liquid and to make a batter with soft dropping consistency. Put into prepared cake tin/s.

Cook in the oven for about 1 hour 20 minutes (checking after 50 minutes), until a skewer inserted into the centre comes out clean. (You will need to reduce the cooking time if cooking in smaller tins.)

Raspberry pudding

DULCIE FRENCH, CENTRAL COAST BRANCH, TAS.

- 1 × 85-g packet raspberry jelly crystals
- 500 g raspberries (fresh or frozen)
- 1 dessertspoon gelatine
- 1 × 375-ml can evaporated milk, chilled
- ice-cream, to serve (optional)

SERVES 6

Boil 2 cups water in a saucepan, add jelly crystals and raspberries and stir until crystals dissolve. Continue to boil for 5 minutes. Remove from heat and add gelatine, stirring until dissolved. Set aside to cool.

Whip evaporated milk to a thick cream, then add jelly mixture (which should have started to set) and whip again. Pour into a serving dish and put in the refrigerator to set. Serve with ice-cream if desired.

Sponge for stewed fruit

NOLA TRELOAR, DEVONPORT BRANCH, TAS.

85 g butter, melted
1 cup milk
vanilla essence, to taste
1 cup self-raising flour
pinch of salt
85 g sugar
1 egg, beaten
500 g hot stewed fruit

SERVES 4–6

Preheat oven to 150°C (fan-forced). Grease a baking dish.

Mix together melted butter, milk and vanilla to taste. Add sifted flour and salt, sugar and egg and mix well.

Place hot stewed fruit in the baking dish and pour batter over. Bake until sponge is light-brown (about 20 minutes).

Apple crumble 1

This apple crumble was all my grandsons ever wanted for dessert at Christmas.

JULIE CHAPPEL, MILLOO BRANCH, VIC.

½ cup self-raising flour
½ cup sugar
½ cup desiccated coconut
55 g butter
3–4 apples, stewed

SERVES 6

Preheat the oven to 190°C. Grease an ovenproof dish.

Combine dry ingredients, then rub in butter to form crumbs. Place warm stewed apples in the ovenproof dish and crumble the coconut mixture over. Bake in the oven until golden-brown. Serve hot or cold.

Apple crumble 2

I make this recipe for the family on cold winter nights.

PHYLLIS HINGSTON, SASSAFRAS/WESLEY VALE BRANCH, TAS.

6 apples, peeled, cored and sliced
3 tablespoons sugar
2 teaspoons butter
3 cloves

crumble topping

2 tablespoons butter
¾ cup self-raising flour
½ cup soft brown sugar

SERVES 5–6

Preheat the oven to 180°C. Grease a pie dish.

Place the apples in a saucepan with the sugar, butter, cloves and 3 tablespoons water and stew until soft. Transfer to the prepared dish.

To make the crumble topping, rub butter into the flour and sugar until mixture resembles breadcrumbs, then sprinkle it over the apples. Bake for 25 minutes, until golden-brown. Serve hot or cold.

Colo's plum pudding

This is my favourite recipe for plum pudding. My mother made it for her first Christmas with my father, 75 years ago. She used dripping and treacle in those days, but I use butter and syrup.

SHIRLEY PLATZ, MIDDLE RIDGE BRANCH, QLD

1 kg mixed dried fruit
½ cup rum or black tea
340 g softened butter
340 g soft brown sugar
5 eggs
½ cup golden syrup
2 tablespoons jam
2 cups plain flour
1 teaspoon bicarbonate of soda
mixed spice, ground cinnamon and nutmeg to taste
2 cups fresh breadcrumbs

SERVES 8

Soak the fruit in the rum or black tea overnight.

The next day, cream the butter with the brown sugar. Beat in the eggs, syrup and jam. Stir in the fruit and rum. Sift together the flour, soda and spices, then mix with the fresh breadcrumbs and add to the fruit mixture. Stir to combine well.

Place mixture in a scalded cloth and boil for 4 hours. Eat hot or cold. (The cooked pudding can be frozen and reheated.)

Caramel pudding

A very easy, popular sweet. Visitors and family have been served this many times.

BETTY LEHMAN, SPREYTON BRANCH, TAS.

1½ cups self-raising flour

⅓ cup white sugar

1½ cups milk

1 cup raisins or mixed dried fruit

2 cups boiling water (I add a bit more to make more topping)

1 cup soft brown sugar

240 g butter

SERVES 6–8

Preheat oven to 180°C. Butter a fairly deep 25-cm × 15-cm ovenproof dish (or a bit bigger).

Mix sifted flour with white sugar, milk and fruit. Place mixture in the prepared dish and pour boiling water over, then sprinkle with the soft brown sugar and add butter (I just put the butter on top in one big lump – the hot water will dissolve it). Bake in the preheated oven for 45 minutes.

Copha cake

For Sunday night family tea we would always have a copha cake.

ELAINE YOUD, DEVONPORT BRANCH, TAS.

230 g icing sugar
1 heaped dessertspoon cocoa
1 egg
vanilla essence, to taste
85 g copha
230 g coffee biscuits (softened by exposure)

MAKES 20–24

Mix the sifted sugar and cocoa with the egg and vanilla. Heat the copha until hot (not boiling) and stir into the mixture. Grease a piece of greaseproof paper and arrange four biscuits end to end on top, then spread some of the copha mixture onto the biscuits. Repeat with more layers of biscuits and copha mixture and until you reach the required size (about five or six layers in total), finishing by covering the top and sides with copha mixture to make a log. Stand in a cool place until set, then cut into slices.

Steamed pudding

At 85 years old, I still often take this steamed pudding to family members and friends for an evening meal – always served with custard and cream. For big family meals I triple the quantity.

AILSA BOND A.M., RIVERSIDE BRANCH, TAS.

55 g softened butter
¼ cup sugar
1 egg, beaten
110 g self-raising flour
¼ cup milk

SERVES 4–6

Cream butter and sugar together, then beat in egg. Gradually add sifted flour and milk, alternately. Put mixture in a greased steamer and place in a saucepan with enough hot water to cover half the steamer. Cook for 1 hour.

Variations

Golden syrup: Add a couple of tablespoons of golden syrup.

Raspberry: Add a couple of tablespoons raspberry jam.

Rainbow pudding children will love: Divide mixture into three and add a few drops cochineal colouring to one third, a tablespoon drinking chocolate powder or cocoa to the second third, and leave the last third plain.

Best-ever sultana cake

This is a very old recipe. The cake keeps well and is very moist.

GLADYS RADFORD, SASSAFRAS/WESLEY VALE BRANCH, TAS.

500 g sultanas
250 g butter, chopped
3 eggs
1 cup sugar
2 teaspoons almond essence
1½ cups plain flour
1 teaspoon baking powder

SERVES 8–14

Preheat oven to 150°C. Grease a 20-cm square or round cake tin.

Place sultanas in a saucepan and cover with cold water, bring to the boil, then drain. Stir in butter and set aside to cool.

Beat together the eggs, sugar and almond essence, then add sultanas. Sift flour with the baking powder and stir into the sultana mixture. Pour into prepared tin and bake for 1½ hours.

Mother's half-hour steamed pudding

NOLA TRELOAR, DEVONPORT BRANCH, TAS.

1 cup milk

1 tablespoon butter

¾ cup sugar

1 cup mixed dried fruit

1 cup self-raising flour

1 level teaspoon bicarbonate of soda

pinch of salt

custard and cream, to serve

SERVES 6

Combine milk, butter, sugar and fruit in a large saucepan and slowly bring to the boil. Remove from the heat and add sifted flour, soda and salt, folding in evenly and gently. Place mixture in a greased bowl and steam for about 30 minutes in boiling water.

Serve with custard and cream.

Quick coconut cake

P. SAUNDERS, SELBOURNE BRANCH, TAS.

1 cup desiccated coconut
1 cup self-raising flour
½ cup sugar
1 cup milk
2 cups icing sugar

SERVES 12

Preheat the oven to 180°C. Grease a loaf tin.

Mix together coconut, sifted flour, sugar and milk (the mixture will be soft). Pour into prepared tin and bake for 45 minutes.

Make plain icing by combining sifted icing sugar with enough water or milk to achieve the desired consistency. Ice cake with plain icing when cold.

Spread cake slices with butter to serve, if desired.

Apple snow

In the post-war time, when supplies were limited, Mum quite often made this very tasty summer dessert for us.

PATRICIA WALKER, GEORGE TOWN BRANCH, TAS.

6 medium-sized apples, peeled, cored and thinly sliced

2 tablespoons caster sugar

1 teaspoon grated lemon zest or a pinch of ground cinnamon

2 egg whites

baked egg custard (page 171) or pouring custard, to serve

SERVES 6

Place apples and 2 tablespoons water in a saucepan. Cover and simmer until soft. Add sugar and stir until sugar is dissolved and mixture is smooth and light. Mix in lemon zest or cinnamon. Transfer to a container and chill thoroughly in the refrigerator.

Beat egg whites until stiff, then fold into the chilled apple mixture. Pile lightly into six individual dishes. Serve at once with custard.

Jelly whip

PHYLLIS HINGSTON, SASSAFRAS/WESLEY VALE BRANCH, TAS.

2 × 85-g packets green jelly crystals

2½ cups boiling water

1 × 375-ml can evaporated milk

cream or ice-cream, to serve

SERVES 6–8

Dissolve jelly crystals in the hot water. Allow to cool and when almost set add the evaporated milk and beat until it thickens. Put into a serving bowl and refrigerate. Serve with cream or ice-cream.

Baked egg custard

PATRICIA WALKER, GEORGE TOWN BRANCH, TAS.

2–3 eggs (depending on size)
2 tablespoons sugar
600 ml milk
3 drops vanilla essence
butter
ground nutmeg, for sprinkling

SERVES 4–6

Preheat the oven to 160°C. Grease a pie dish with a little butter.

Beat eggs and sugar in a mixing bowl. Warm milk in a small saucepan. When milk is warm, stir in vanilla, then add to the egg mixture and mix well. Pour custard into the prepared dish. Dot with butter and sprinkle with ground nutmeg. Place the pie dish into a slightly larger baking dish and pour hot water into the larger dish until about 2.5 cm deep. Place in the oven and bake for 30–45 minutes, until the top is lightly browned. (The custard is cooked when a knife inserted into the centre comes out clean, and no custard runs out.)

Jelly cheesecake

This recipe was given to me by my aunt, who said it was her aunt's recipe. She has made it for many of our family functions in the past.

KARINA ZANCHETTA, GEORGE TOWN BRANCH, TAS.

whipped cream and grated lemon zest, to serve

base

230 g Nice biscuits, crushed

150 g butter or margarine, melted

filling

110 g cream cheese

¾ cup sugar

1 × 375-ml can evaporated milk, chilled

1 × 85-g packet lemon jelly crystals

1 cup boiling water

1 tablespoon lemon juice

SERVES 8

Preheat oven to 150°C. Grease a 20-cm springform tin.

To make the base, mix biscuit crumbs with melted butter, then press into prepared tin. Cook in the oven for about 10 minutes, then put in the fridge to cool.

To make the filling, beat the cream cheese and sugar until combined. In a separate bowl beat the evaporated milk until very thick. Add cream cheese mixture and beat in. Dissolve jelly in the hot water and allow to cool. When cold, add lemon juice to the jelly, then add jelly to the cream cheese mixture and stir well. Pour into the tin on top of the biscuit base. Refrigerate until set.

Spread whipped cream over the cake and decorate with grated lemon zest.

Boiled fruit pudding

This was the recipe I made for my first Christmas as a family, with my husband and eldest daughter. It was made by my mother-in-law every Sunday lunch (except during the apple season when we had apple pie).

MARION SPAULDING, HIGHCROFT/STORMLEA BRANCH, TAS.

- 2 tablespoons softened butter or margarine
- ½ cup sugar
- 1 egg
- 1 cup mixed dried fruit (raisins, sultanas, currants – you can also add almonds, cherries and mixed peel for a richer pudding)
- 1 cup plain flour
- 1 teaspoon bicarbonate of soda
- 2 tablespoons milk
- custard, cream and ice-cream, to serve

SERVES 6

Cream butter and sugar, then beat in egg. Add fruit and sifted flour and soda. Add a little milk to make a soft, but not runny, mixture.

Scald a pudding cloth and sprinkle with sugar. Place mixture in the centre and tie very tightly, allowing a little room for rising. Place in a large saucepan or boiler with a saucer in the bottom and half-fill with boiling water. Boil for 2 hours.

Serve with custard, cream and ice-cream.

Apple caramel scrolls

EILEEN McMULLEN, RANELAGH BRANCH, TAS.

- 1 cup self-raising flour
- 1 dessertspoon sugar
- about ⅓ cup milk
- 1 cup cold sweetened stewed apple
- ground cinnamon, for sprinkling
- custard or cream, to serve

caramel sauce

- 4 heaped tablespoons soft brown sugar
- 1 tablespoon butter

SERVES 4–6

Preheat the oven to 200°C. Grease a pie dish.

Combine sifted flour and sugar and add enough milk to make a firm dough. Roll dough out until about 4 mm thick and approximately 10-cm × 30-cm in size. Spread apple over the dough and sprinkle with cinnamon. Roll the pastry up, starting with a long side, to make a long log. Cut the log into six slices (each about 5-cm wide) and place flat-side down in the pie dish.

To make the sauce, combine sugar and butter in a small saucepan with 1 tablespoon water. Bring slowly to the boil and cook for 1 minute. Pour sauce over the scrolls in the pie dish and bake for 15 minutes.

Serve with custard or cream.

Baked jam roll

This dessert is always popular when the family comes over for a Sunday lunch or dinner.

JUDY PRATT, DARWIN BRANCH, NT

1 cup self-raising flour
pinch of salt
1 tablespoon butter or margarine
about 1 teaspoon milk
jam, for spreading
custard or cream, to serve

glaze

¼ cup sugar
1 tablespoon butter
1 cup boiling water

SERVES 6–8

Preheat the oven 180°C. Grease a rectangular baking dish (I use a 25-cm × 16-cm Pyrex dish).

Sift flour and salt into a bowl, add butter and a little milk and mix together to make a dough. Roll dough out into a rectangle shape and spread with jam. Roll up and place in prepared dish.

To make the glaze, combine sugar, butter and boiling water in a saucepan, stirring over low heat until sugar has dissolved. Pour syrup over the pudding and bake for about 30 minutes.

Serve with custard or cream.

Coconut ice cake

My mother made this for me and my two brothers as a treat for our birthdays. I made it for my own children when they were small, and I still make it for special occasions.

MARY HANSLOW, ORIELTON BRANCH, TAS.

85 g softened butter
½ cup sugar
1 egg
1 cup plain flour
½ teaspoon baking powder
1 cup desiccated coconut

topping
2 cups sugar
½ cup milk
1 teaspoon butter
1 teaspoon vanilla essence
cochineal colouring
½ cup desiccated coconut

SERVES 10–12

Preheat the oven to 180°C. Grease a Swiss roll tin.

Cream butter and sugar, then add egg, sifted flour and baking powder, and coconut. Mix well. Put in prepared tin and bake until golden-brown. Remove and set aside to cool.

To make topping, boil sugar and milk for 4 minutes, then add butter, vanilla, a few drops of cochineal and the coconut. Beat until smooth and thick. Spread on top of cooled base.

Conversions

(All conversions are approximate)

Oven temperatures

°C (Celsius)	°F (Fahrenheit)
120	250
150	300
160	320
170	340
175	350
180	355
190	375
200	390
220	430

Cake tin measures

cm (centimetres)	in (inches)
2.5	1
5	2
8	3
10	4
13	5
15	6
18	7
20	8
23	9
25	10
28	11
36	14

Tip: *To test if a cake is cooked, insert a thin skewer into the centre of the cake; if it comes out clean, the cake is ready.*

Weights

g (grams)	oz (ounces)
30	1
55–60	2
90	3
100	3½
110	4
125	4½
150	5
200	7
250	9
300	10½
340	12
400	14
450	16 (1 lb)
500	1lb 1½ oz

Liquid measures

ml (millilitres)	fl oz (fluid ounces – UK)
50	1¾
100	3½
200	7
300	10½
400	14
500	17½
600	1 pt 1 fl oz
700	1 pt 5 fl oz
1000 (1 litre)	1 pt 15 fl oz

Index

PENGUIN BOOKS

Published by the Penguin Group
Penguin Group (Australia)
250 Camberwell Road, Camberwell, Victoria 3124, Australia
(a division of Pearson Australia Group Pty Ltd)

New York Toronto London Dublin New Delhi Auckland Johannesburg

Penguin Books Ltd, Registered Offices: 80 Strand, London, WC2R 0RL, England

First published by Penguin Group (Australia) in association with the Country Women's Association of Australia, 2009

10 9 8 7 6 5 4 3 2 1

Text and cover design by Claire Tice & Marley Flory © Penguin Group (Australia), 2009
Photography by Julie Renouf
Food styling by Lee Blaylock
Typeset in Avenir by Post Pre-press Group, Brisbane, Queensland
Scanning and separations by Splitting Image P/L, Clayton, Victoria
Printed in China by Everbest Printing Co. Ltd

National Library of Australia
Cataloguing-in-Publication data:

Country Women's Association family meals.
ISBN: 978 0 14 320233 2 (pbk.)
Includes index.
Cookery.
Other Authors/Contributors:
Country Women's Association of Australia

641.5

penguin.com.au